The WayOut Bunch®

Created by
Jenny Tulip and Dawn Smith

The Way Out Bunch books feature
genuinely endangered living animals.
The information in each book is collated
from known facts about them.

© Green Arc Creations Ltd

All paper used comes from sustainably managed forests

I'm Curious Cat on an adventure to see
what the animal within these pages can be.
So let's read together and have a good look
and we shall find out by the end of this book.

Curious Cat is off to explore Pakistan
"Help me choose the Pakistani flag,
and I will wear it on my hat."

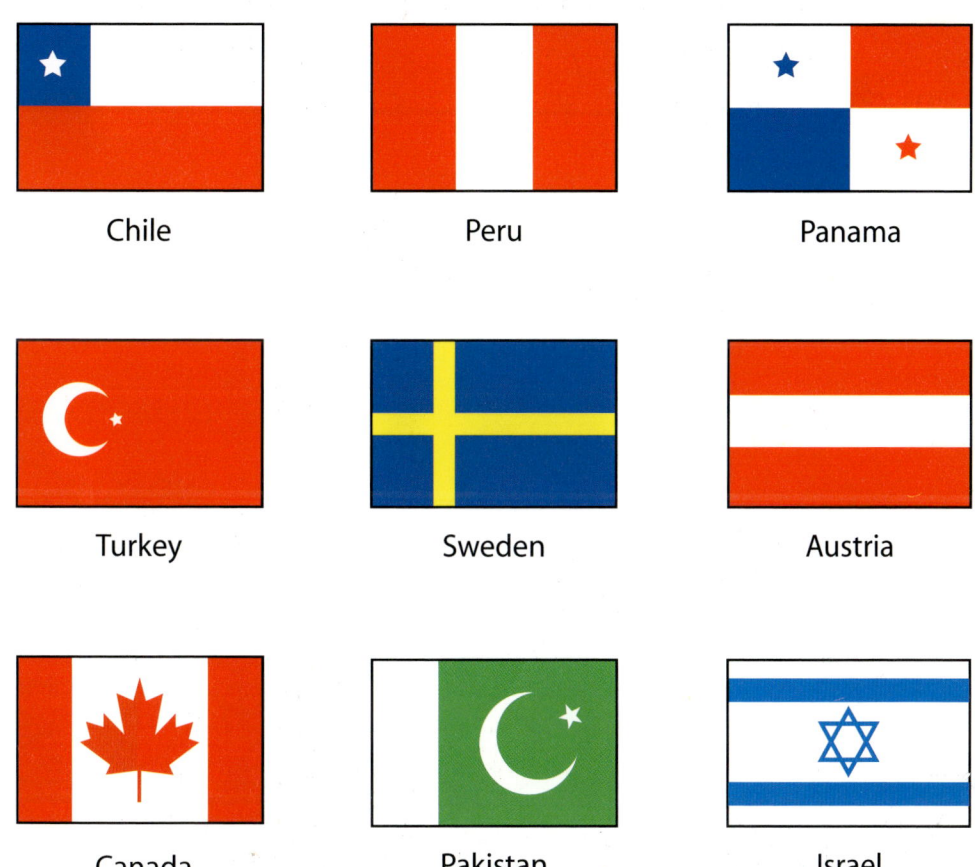

I warm the cold air with my pink and black nose
And my keen sense of smell
keeps my lunch on its toes.

My eyes bright and green
on the look out for prey.
Fast food is my diet but not every day.

I have big furry paws for walking on snow,
they keep my feet warm wherever I go.

My tail's very furry, it's the biggest and best,
For balance when running and
warmth when I rest.

"Sometimes it is very cold where this animal lives.
What clothes would you wear to keep warm?"

My strong teeth and jaws
are a tough act to beat
For crunching on bones
and munching on meat.

My favourite foods are hares, goats and sheep.
I can creep up upon them
or pounce, chase and leap!

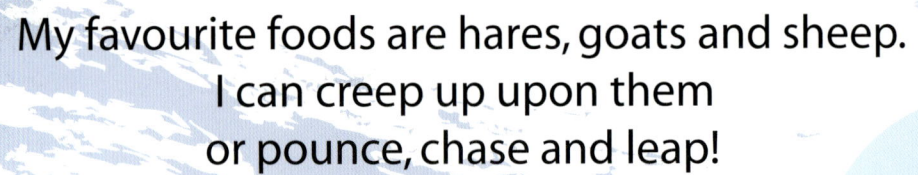

"What does this animal like to eat?
Can you remember?"

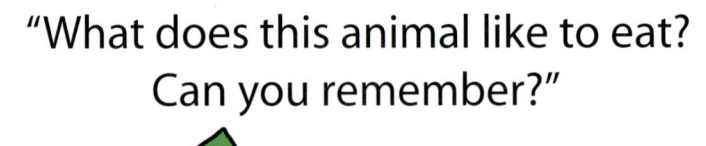

I'm shy and elusive and not easily found.
My spotty grey coat's like the rocks all around.

"Do you know what I could be?
Let's turn the page and we shall see."

Yes, I'm a Snow Leopard, as you probably knew; my fur, paws and tail are a very big clue.

Did you know.....

Humans need to wear thick boots when they go out in the snow but the Snow Leopard has thick fur on the soles of their paws which keeps their feet warm

Their large paws act like snow shoes and stop them from sinking in deep snow.

They also allow them to run and jump on sharp rocks and boulders when chasing prey.

With short front legs and long hind legs, Snow Leopards are very agile and can leap up to 15m between rocky crags in the mountains where they live.

The Snow Leopard's thick grey fur is marked with spots and rosettes which make them almost impossible to see in the wild.

Their tail is nearly as long as their body and is used to help them balance when chasing prey.

They wrap their tail around their body and face for warmth when resting.

Snow Leopards hunt a variety of prey, including animals up to three times their own weight.

They live in the Himalayan mountains of central Asia, between 3000 and 4500 m above sea level.

They are endangered because human beings are moving into their natural habitat, forcing them to move higher into the mountains where it is colder and there is less to eat.

They were often hunted for their beautiful coats. As an endangered animal the Snow Leopard is now a protected species, and anyone caught hunting them faces a heavy fine.

If you would like to find out more information on endangered animals and how to help them, visit these websites:

WWF-UK - www.wwf.org.uk
The Edge programme - www.edgeofexistence.org
ARKive, images of life on Earth - www.arkive.org
A percentage of our profits will be donated to relevant charities.